Antonio Rosmini

Priest, Founder of the
Institute of Charity

by
J.B. Midgley

*All booklets are published thanks to the
generous support of the members of the
Catholic Truth Society*

CATHOLIC TRUTH SOCIETY
PUBLISHERS TO THE HOLY SEE

Contents

In piam memoriam
Hazel Midgley
Returned to God, 8th May 2014

All rights reserved. First published 2015 by The Incorporated Catholic Truth Society, 40-46 Harleyford Road London SE11 5AY Tel: 020 7640 0042 Fax: 020 7640 0046. © 2015 The Incorporated Catholic Truth Society.

ISBN 978 1 78469 058 8

Introduction

In March 1999, Father Peter-Hans Kolvenbach, former Father General of the Society of Jesus, wrote a gracious article titled, "Rosmini, a Prophet for the Third Millennium". In this he said, "From 1955, the first centenary of Rosmini's death, we have experienced a re-flowering of interest in him who is a 'European thinker', and a courageous witness of the mystery of the Church. The Jesuits rejoice in the process of beatification that has begun and pledges itself to it wholeheartedly. It is a sign of the new times that give reason to hope that Rosmini, an example to us all, can play a fundamental role at the dawn of the twenty-first century." The process of beatification did indeed come to a happy conclusion when Pope Benedict XVI declared Antonio "Venerable" on 3rd June 2007 and his beatification was proclaimed five months later on 18th November.

In the first encyclical of his pontificate, Pope Benedict observed that "the lives of the saints are not limited to their earthly biographies, but continue being and working in God after death. They do not withdraw from men, but rather become truly close to them." Like the Blessed Virgin Mary, they love every generation with a benevolence that results from "intimate union with God, through which the soul is totally pervaded by him – a condition which enables those who have drunk from the fountains of God's love to become in their turn a fountain from which 'flow rivers of living water'" (*Deus Caritas Est*, n.42).

The story of Antonio Rosmini-Serbati, founder of the Institute of Charity and the Sisters of Providence, illustrates the essential character of Catholic life. Though prayer adds nothing to his perfection, God wants those he has created to talk to him, and bestows the grace to respond to his invitation, not least in the company of the saints whose charity, power and intercession do not diminish with the passing of time. We can confidently call upon the eager assistance of Blessed Antonio, a shining light for our times who understands the present needs and aspirations of God's People.

Rosminian Spirituality

In 1970, members of the Institute of Charity, inspired by their Founder's philosophy, intellect, and devotion, compiled and published an anthology entitled *Rosminian Spirituality*. This is based upon Antonio's writings and reflects his wish that his brothers and sisters should have a meditation book to support prayerful consideration of the entire Gospel, help an appreciation of the spirit of the Institute, and serve the spiritual aspirations of the whole Christian community. A selection aimed at a general readership has been made below; the texts have been slightly adapted.

The world awaiting Antonio

The eighteenth century was not a happy time for the continent of Europe, especially in France where the reigns of Louis XIV and Louis XV witnessed various attempts by secular and clerical leaders to separate the local Church from the control of Rome. To these were added tension between Church and State arising from the growing nationalism, secularism and atheism with which Pope Pius VI had been forced to contend since his election in 1775. Lavish expenditure in high places and extensive privileges for the rich inflicted crippling taxation on the working and rural classes who were driven to angry despair. When the situation further deteriorated, a beleaguered populace rose in protest and the French Revolution erupted in 1789. The Revolutionaries adopted an anti-clerical programme that led to the closure of churches unless they were served by priests who swore allegiance to a State Church, and any who refused to accept the Civil Constitution of the Clergy were deported or executed. The more fortunate went into hiding, and persecuted members of religious orders had to disguise themselves or escape to less dangerous places in Europe.

When the Revolution's Reign of Terror ended in in 1791 with the execution of Robespierre, the rule of the French Republic passed to a group called the Directory that held sway until Napoleon seized power. He set about destroying ecclesiastical principalities, invaded the Papal States, and imposed arduous terms of peace on Pope Pius. Bonaparte demanded that the Pope surrender a substantial section of territory along with precious works of art and manuscripts, and left him with no alternative but to give recognition to the French Republic. Pope Pius VI was eventually deposed as head of state, driven from Rome in 1799, and died in exile when Antonio Rosmini was only two years of age.

"Enlightenment"

The Benedictine Pope Pius VII ascended the papal throne the following year, and the first major responsibility he undertook was to help the Church come to terms with the new philosophical, political and scientific movement remembered as the "Enlightenment". This was the creation of European philosophers including Diderot, Rousseau and Kant who, intent on reforming society, developed and popularised the earlier thinking of Newton, Hobbs, Locke, Descartes and Spinoza. It was characterised by a confident assessment of human reason, an optimistic view of human nature, passionate advocacy of the individual's freedom, and an abhorrence of tradition, religion, the supernatural, and any authority that was not founded on what they saw

The Human Person

'Man is a person created by God as an intelligent, free individual whom he calls to collaborate with him in his own formation. The person is an intelligent, substantive individual in so far as he has within himself a supreme, active and incommunicable principle.'

(Fr Antonio Rosmini)

The True Measure of Personality

'To speak of "person", is to refer to the supreme principle that gives true worth to Man, and to which we accord esteem. If we speak of a "good person" we are not assessing his intellect, talent or physique but his moral value that is the true measure of his personality. Christianity clarifies what we know instinctively, that our moral capacity is sterile when separated from absolute good. The phrase: "I am free" has no significance unless completed with the words "to do good".'

(Fr Antonio Rosmini)

as "reason". Though it tended to have more influence on Protestantism, it did produce a climate that stimulated Catholic leaders to turn attention to education including that of the clergy, to revive Biblical and theological scholarship, and eradicate some superstitions masquerading as religion. The resultant developments in Catholic theology sought to accommodate the implications of scientific and technological progress, and the impact on social reform of the humanitarian ideals of tolerance, equality and freedom.

Signs of Hope

The Concordat of 1802 between France and the Papacy brought some relief. Napoleon now allowed the Pope to re-establish the Catholic Church in France but only on condition he appoint a new hierarchy and accept that the Church was subordinate to the State. The relationship remained problematic, but Napoleon found it politically expedient to make some helpful acknowledgement of Papal authority. Pius VII was now in a stronger position to combat "enlightened" secular modernity, and refresh the clergy's education with emphasis on their pastoral responsibilities. He made Rome a centre of culture by restoring old and opening new museums, and building schools to expand the education system. When Napoleon decided to crown himself Emperor in 1804, the Pope was at least given the courtesy of an invitation and attended the ceremony in Paris.

"Ultramontanism"

Despite persecution, bloodshed and terror, the Revolution was to bring some benefit to the Church in France. Previously closely aligned with the French throne, her feudal, hierarchical and mediaeval characteristics were now so diminished that clergy and faithful looked instead to Rome and the Pope for protection. This change of heart led to the attitude known as "Ultramontanism" meaning dependence on the City "beyond the mountains" (the Alps, that is). Europe as a whole welcomed the Church's deliverance from wealth and power as "a grace of destitution" that inspired a re-alignment of her fundamental mission to preach the Gospel and serve the people in fidelity to Apostolic teaching. There emerged a new-found enthusiasm for the traditional and intellectual values of the Church as the mother of art and guardian of patriotism, and the Romantic movement in literature and art brought a renewed appreciation of emotion, intuition, individualism, and history that balanced the Enlightenment's emphasis on classicism and reason. This generated a respectful re-evaluation of the attitudes and values of previous eras, but also a cautious response towards speculative theology, and a reliance on Rome for authoritative answers to questions relating to faith and morals. This situation would have a bearing on Antonio's philosophy and his enduring contribution to the life of the Church.

The Human Person and the Will of God

'A calling to perfection assumes intelligence in the created person who is called, and finite intelligences are drawn to perfection because the Infinite Creator already possesses every perfection. So, using his gifts the human person searches for perfection as a means of fulfilling God's will.'

(Fr Antonio Rosmini)

Antonio's arrival

For several centuries, the Rosmini-Serbati family had lived in Rovereto, a town in northern Italy that had been part of the Austrian Empire since 1509 and, though ruled from Vienna, had faithfully retained its Italian heritage. The business of silk manufacture had made the family rich, and allowed them to enjoy the privileged life of minor aristocracy. Antonio Rosmini-Serbati was born here on 24th March 1797, and was baptized the following day. His father, Pier Modesto, has been described as admirably civilised though rather strict, and his mother, Giovanna dei Conti Formenti di Riva, as gracefully warm-hearted and educated. Their first child was Antonio's sister Gioseffa Margherita, who one day become a nun, and later they would be joined by a brother, Giuseppe, who was to prove something of a difficult character.

The young scholar

Antonio was nurtured in a contented atmosphere of devout and practical Catholicism to which his uncle Ambrogio, who lived in the family house, made a valuable contribution. Early on, this skilled architect, artist and scholar recognised his nephew's intellectual gifts, and encouraged his keen desire for knowledge. His interest was soon rewarded because

Antonio could read and write by the time he was five, not least because he wanted to know more of the Bible and the lives of the saints. When he reached school age his parents were happy to enrol him in local schools; good primary and secondary education there was enriched by his own wide reading. He was fortunate in having a library at home that gave him access to the teaching of the Fathers of the Church, for whom he developed a profound reverence evident in his own future writings (which also reveal an encyclopaedic knowledge of the Holy Scriptures). He benefited from additional tuition from an inspirational priest, Don Pietro Orsi, whose teaching of philosophy so inspired him that he began to study Kant, Hegel, and Locke. In time, he would attempt to correct their theories, relying particularly on St Augustine and St Thomas Aquinas whom he recognised as among the greatest intellects in the history of the Church.

Vocation to the Priesthood

In August 1816, Antonio sat his final exams at secondary school and was awarded the grade of "eminence" in all subjects, with a written evaluation that testified to his "tremendously keen intelligence." Three years earlier, when only sixteen, he had written in his 1813 personal diary, "This was a year of grace for me. God opened my mind to many things and I knew that there was no other wisdom but in God". At first, his parents were none too thrilled when he told them of his intention to devote his life

I have chosen you.

'God gives us the grace to cooperate with his Son in his work of Redemption and we need not allow our faults to place obstacles in the way of such divine mercy. He reserves to himself everything that relates to perfection in the moral order, but from all eternity has chosen to use human instruments as ministers of that order. As we attend to our own souls he diffuses his goodness through us so that his plans are fulfilled through us. The more you trust and hope in God, the greater and more frequent will be the graces you receive through him. Do not let your weakness frighten you but rather consider it a trophy for the glory of God who wishes to use instruments that might otherwise be useless. The lives of the Apostles and their successors reveal their constancy in difficulties and unceasing confidence in God, and Our Lord asks that we unite our sufferings to his so that his merits are applied to the souls of all. In this way, we share in his glory and join him as co-redeemers of the world.'

(*Fr Antonio Rosmini*)

to God as a priest. After all, he was the elder son and more likely to carry on the family name and have a successful life in the world than his recalcitrant brother Giuseppe. When they failed to dissuade him, Pier Modesto, reasonably hoping that his son would achieve eminence in the Church, suggested he should study in Rome, but Antonio was not interested in position or privilege. After preliminary studies in Pavia he went to read theology and Canon Law in the University of Padua where his namesake, the Franciscan St Anthony, had taught in the thirteenth century.

Ordination

During three years at Padua Antonio distinguished himself and won an enviable reputation. When he had completed his studies, he returned to Rovereto to prepare for Holy Orders, and on 21st April 1821 the Bishop of Chioggia ordained him to the priesthood. Those who assisted at his first Mass included a very young John Bosco, the future saint and founder of the Salesian Order, and all were moved by the great devotion with which the new priest celebrated Mass. Antonio then returned home for a period of prayer and meditation, during which time he also visited Verona with his sister Margherita. There he met the Marchioness, St Maddalena of Canossa, who had founded the Daughters of Charity. She suggested that he might establish a religious institute for men to complement her own and, though he thought the time not quite right, her invitation was soon to meet with a splendid response.

Education and personality

Those who guide aspirants to the priesthood and the religious life to form true Christian personality will not forget the natural virtues that assist the general formation of personality that embraces keeping one's resolutions, persevering in the good work identified, frankness, loyalty, and fidelity to one's word. Respect for these virtues will inspire confidence and a love of the other supernatural virtues that form true personality. (*Fr Antonio Rosmini*)

Early works and Papal commission

Antonio had already commenced his literary works in 1820 with a book, *On Christian Education*, that he wrote for his sister Margherita who by now had opened a school for orphans. This was soon followed by *In Praise of Saint Philip Neri*, a *History of Love*, and an *Essay on Happiness*. In 1822, he returned to Padua to receive his doctorate in theology and Canon Law and, by now, his piety, personality and burgeoning academic renown had attracted the admiring interest of Cardinal Ladislao Pyrcher, the Patriarch of Venice, who took him to Rome in 1823 and introduced him to the Pope, Pius VII, who was similarly impressed and asked him to reform philosophy in a Catholic context. "Remember", he told him, "you must attend to writing books rather than busy yourself with the affairs of the active life. You handle logic well, and we need writers like you." With relevance for succeeding generations, Antonio was to demonstrate the positive interrelationship of faith, theology, philosophy, and science. While in Rome he also met the Camaldolese Abbot, Bartolomeo Cappellari, a stalwart supporter of Papal sovereignty and infallibility, about which he had in 1799 written an influential defence. An immediate friendship was forged that was to be significant in days to come. The young priest also impressed Cardinal Ercole Consalvi, the Vatican Secretary of State who, after Napoleon's downfall, negotiated the re-establishment of the Papal States and restored the Papacy's prestige at the Congress of Vienna (1814-1815), after the end of the Napoleonic Wars.

A new Pope

Pius VII was eighty-one and had been Pope for twenty-three eventful years when he died on 20th July 1823. In the aftermath of the secularising Enlightenment he had both opposed modernity and encouraged tolerance of contemporary thought; he had expanded missions to Asia, and revived priestly education and pastoral commitment. He had entered into concordats with Italy and France, but Napoleon ordered his arrest when he bravely resisted assaults on the Church and excommunicated all "robbers of Peter's patrimony". From 1809 to 1814, while held prisoner in Genoa and Fontainebleau, he reverted to the life of a monk and was admired for his dignity in suffering. He returned to Rome after Napoleon's defeat. Antonio immediately wrote and preached his "Panegyric for Pius VII", but publication was delayed for eight years because the Austrian government said it contained signs of excessive Italian patriotism. In fact, like others in the early years of the nineteenth century, Antonio recoiled from the excesses of the French Revolution and objected to state interference in religious affairs.

Sacramental Life

When God the Creator deigned to become a creature like us, he humbled himself, and the more so because the contact is with a creature who has fallen below its normal level through sin. Christ's revitalising power comes to us in the sacraments, particularly the Eucharist in which the bread and wine are substantially united with him. In the mystery of the sacraments, we are able to understand that his life and presence in us is real, and his infinite charity becomes for us a spring of boundless confidence, as well as an obligation to respond with gratitude and awe. In this regard, we are able to see that married life and celibacy, for example, have a common call for dedication and perseverance, but are comforted to know that in the sacraments of Matrimony and Ordination the Lord is always there with his helping presence. The Sacraments have a social function and visibly clothe themselves with an exterior life that gives the sensible signs of invisible grace, and unites Christians in external activity. The Eucharist has pride of place as an instrument of communication, because the one Bread that nourishes all offers evidence of unity in one Body, and enables a better response to the duty of charity that supports individual members and their mutual harmony. (*Fr Antonio Rosmini*)

Antonio's health declines

Pius was succeeded by Pope Leo XII, a less popular figure whose election was supported by conservative cardinals. Leo dismissed Cardinal Consalvi whom he considered too liberal, condemned religious toleration and Freemasonry, reinforced the *Index of Forbidden Books* and the Holy Office, re-established a feudal aristocracy in the Papal States, and again confined Jews to ghettos. Antonio returned to Rovereto where he devoted himself to philosophy and especially to the study of St Thomas Aquinas. In 1826, he went to Milan to continue his research. He published on many subjects, including the origin of ideas and certitude, the nature of the human soul, ethics, the relationship between Church and State, the philosophy of law, metaphysics, grace, Original Sin, the Sacraments and education, all of which won Pope Leo's wholehearted support. However, he had to admit to a friend, "I wish I could put a break on overwork. My health is obviously suffering because of it. I can see this plainly but am driven along. How much greater than the pleasure of the body is that of the mind." The year 1826 was also important for him because his friend Abbot Cappellari was elevated to the College of Cardinals and became Prefect of the Congregation for the Propagation of the Faith (*Propaganda Fide*).

Grace

'God unites himself to us in the action called grace through which a measure of the divine is infused into the soul. "If a man loves me, he will keep my word, and my Father will love him and we shall come to him and make our abode with him." The divine action of grace continues in the soul giving it a stable energy and imparting a new power to do what otherwise not be possible' (cf. *Jn* 14:23)

(*Fr Antonio Rosmini*).

The Institute of Charity

Principles of Conduct and the Constitution

Antonio records that on 10th December 1825, after replying to a typically encouraging letter from Maddalena of Canossa, he came up with a plan for his religious order. With her practical help and the support of Father John Loewenbruck, a priest from German Lorraine, he founded the Institute of Charity, often called the Rosminians. On Ash Wednesday, 20th February 1828, he began to write the Institute's *Constitutions* in which he incorporated two principles of conduct. The first he described as the "principle of passivity" that was the foundation of his spirituality and became the Institute's special charism. It recommends that members make personal sanctification their first priority, because this is always pleasing to God. Then, before undertaking any work of charity on their own initiative, they await the manifestation of his will which, when known, should receive their wholehearted response. The second was the "principle of indifference" or impartiality, in which, once God's will is apparent, the charitable work of love is undertaken regardless of personal preference or reluctance. It was on such principles that the Institute's *Rule* would be based. Rosmini later told one of his brethren, "The *Constitutions are* not my work;

they did not come from my mind. The plan of the Institute was given to me without my having studied it. I saw it one morning presented to me in a moment, wholly as you see it described."

Further Papal support

In November 1828, Antonio made another visit to Rome because he wanted to assure himself that his philosophical writings and the foundation of the Institute were in accord with God's will. In the remaining three months of his life, Pope Leo encouraged the Institute's consolidation and the continuation of its founder's philosophical work. Pope Leo died in February 1829 and was succeeded by Pope Pius VIII, who returned to the spirit and policies of Pius VII and treated the more liberal movements with some caution. He too rejoiced in the Institute's birth and told Antonio, "It is God's will that you should write books and that is where your vocation lies. The Church greatly needs writers to win people to the faith by the use of reason." Antonio's immediately responded with his *Maxims of Christian Perfection* which brilliantly summarise his ascetical teaching, and his first great philosophical work, *A New Essay on the Origin of Ideas*, which won wide acclaim for its fresh approach to contemporary philosophy. In the autumn of 1830, the Rule of the Institute of Charity was inaugurated in its first house, which had been opened at Monte Calvario near Domo d'Ossola in Piedmont, at the

Universal charity

'Of its nature, charity is universal and intends every good as far as possible. Although God has given us a heart that aspires to all good things, our limitations require that we must not waste effort by undertaking more good works than are capable of accomplishment. Often a greater good may be effected by a group's cooperative endeavour than by the same people working separately. On our own, we might think that we have not done much good but we must remember that God is still pleased with our attempt especially when we have tried to contribute to a communal effort to do good. The greatest proof of the virtues of our religion and the most convincing even to its enemies is the charity it inspires in its faithful followers. For this reason, Jesus Christ wanted the commandment of love which he echoes not in our ears but in our hearts to be the characteristic mark of his disciples in all its beauty.'

(Fr Antonio Rosmini)

foot of the Alps. For some time, Antonio had wondered if he himself should be a member of the Institute, and finally concluded that God wished him to be with his brethren, a decision in keeping with his belief that the Institute was not his own work but of divine inspiration. Pius VIII's brief twenty month papacy ended in November and he was succeeded on 2nd February 1831 by Antonio's friend Cardinal Cappellari, who took the name Gregory XVI.

Morality activated in love

'Every moral act begins and ends in each individual and is expressed in Our Lord's exhortation to "love God above all things and our neighbour as ourselves". Because society is composed of persons, humans are fulfilled in the love and charity of social life. Persons, then, are capable of the reciprocal respect upon which society is based, and they promote the benefit of society and the individual, a concept that is applicable to the Mystical Body of Christ.'

(Fr Antonio Rosmini)

The Apostolate flourishes

The speed at which saints undertake and accomplish what God wants them to do can be awe-inspiring. Members of the Institute could be either priests or religious brothers, devoted to the pastoral care of parishes and parishioners, to the ministries of preaching, education of youth, and universal works of material, spiritual and intellectual charity. They were asked "to embrace with all the desire of their souls every work of charity without arbitrary limitation to any particular branch, undertaking all that should be required of them of which they should be capable." It is a measure of Antonio's inspiring leadership that many men of learning and sanctity joined him and, in due course, to their numbers would be added the Rosminian Sisters of Providence whose *Rule* is also permeated with his spirituality. The opening of houses in Trent, Rovereto, Verona, Stresa and Turin followed that in Monte Calvario so that, by 1832, the Institute was firmly established in northern Italy. Their priestly ministry and works of pastoral charity had expanded to include giving retreats, visiting the sick and imprisoned, writing, conducting missions abroad, and administering an academy dedicated to the study of the works of St Thomas Aquinas. The speed of this expansion demonstrates an unwavering trust in Providence.

Criticism of Antonio's writings

No sooner was the Institute of Charity achieving success than its founder was attacked, not least by some Jesuits, who objected to his writings and even accused him of copying from their constitutions when composing his own. His *Treatise on Moral Conscience* was harshly criticised, and he was called "a heretic of the worst kind". This was the more hurtful because he greatly admired the Jesuits, some of whom had previously praised his devoted work and ideals. It has been suggested that they were still sensitive about their suppression in 1773 by Pope Clement XIV; this suppression was the result of political pressure from the Catholic powers of France, Spain, Portugal and Naples. The Society had survived in Poland and Lithuania until its restoration by Pius VII in 1814 but now, perhaps, some members resented the esteem in which the new Institute was already held. Antonio asked his friend Cardinal Castracane to intercede for him with the Pope and offered to correct any of his writings that were found unacceptable. Gregory XVI imposed silence on both parties but this only resulted in an uneasy and temporary truce.

The Institute comes to the British Isles

From 1834 to 1835, Father Antonio himself took charge of the parish in Rovereto much to the delight and consolation of his parishioners. Pope Gregory then entrusted him with responsibility for the Abbey of Saint Michael of Chiusa in Piedmont and also asked him to arrange a mission to England that had been requested by the English Vicars Apostolic following Catholic Emancipation in 1829. In response to the Pope's request and in obedience to Antonio, Father Luigi Gentili IC arrived in England in 1835 and stayed with the Trelawney family in Cornwall, before establishing a base at Prior Park College near Bath. He immediately began successful preaching missions and worked tirelessly until his death in Dublin in 1854. In addition to their dedicated evangelisation, they introduced the Roman collar to England and the wearing of the religious habit in public. They revived the use of the scapular, and introduced the practice of the Forty Hours of prayer before the Blessed Sacrament solemnly exposed, as well as promoting May devotions to Our Blessed Lady, public processions, novena prayers, and the blessing of throats on 3rd February, the feast of the fourth-century martyr St Blaise (who is credited with healing a boy who was on the point of death because a fishbone was stuck in his throat).

The Institute is approved

On 20th December 1838, after some clarification concerning the Vow of Religious Poverty, Pope Gregory validated the Institute of Charity and its *Constitutions*, and on 25th March 1839, the Feast of the Annunciation, the Vows of the Institute were professed by twenty priests in Italy and six in England - at Spetisbury in Dorset, and at Prior Park. Six months later, in September, the Apostolic Letter *In Sublimi* formally approved the Institute with its *Rule* and appointed Antonio Superior and Provost General for life. A novitiate was opened in Stresa on Lake Maggiore and, in due course, the work of the Institute spread from Italy to France, New Zealand, Kenya, Tanzania, India, Venezuela, America and, not least, to England, Ireland and Wales.

Pope Gregory XVI died on 1st June 1846. He had exercised caution when evaluating liberal thinking in politics, theology, and papal government, and tried to protect the independence of the Church by preserving the Papal States (where, incidentally, he banned railways as dangerous modern inventions). He had co-ordinated the activities of the Church, especially her preaching the Gospel in missionary lands, and centralised her administration within the Holy See. Blessed Pius IX, "Pio Nono", was elected a fortnight later and his reign of thirty-two years would prove to be the longest thus far.

Teaching Christian Doctrine

'One of the greatest sources of modern incredulity is the sophism: "priests act badly, therefore the religion they teach is false". The young should be enabled to receive noble ideas about Divine Providence without being scandalised by events. Remember that it is Christ's doctrine that you are teaching not your own. You should choose exact words to express doctrines of faith without adding personal, complicated ideas. Ideally, doctrinal and moral teaching is best in conjunction with sacred history so that revealed truths give acceptable guidance with added conviction. Let the aim of teaching, therefore, be the love of Spirit and Truth offered in the Scriptures. The teaching of Christ's Church is nourished and guided by the sacred books in which our heavenly Father lovingly meets and speaks to his children. So great is the power of his word that it is the support of the Church, the strength of her children's faith, the nourishment of their souls, and the pure, continuing source of their spiritual life.'

(*Fr Antonio Rosmini*)

Loving kindness

Antonio did not allow the volume of work to distract him from a life of prayer to which he devoted at least five hours every day, all the while considering himself very ordinary. He was motivated by obedience, self-denial and a desire to serve others according to God's will, not his own. He was so alert to what he considered his failings that on 6th August 1846, the Feast of the Transfiguration, he wrote in his diary, "Lord, I live a lie; enfold me in truth." Yet, his writings on charity are unequalled and it is no surprise that he named his order the Institute of Charity. He understood God's love being poured out upon creation and applied to the good works we attempt for the salvation of souls. He wrote: "All our actions must be love, whether applied to temporal or intellectual life, or moral values and holiness which is the life of every other life, and finds its fullness in the Love that is its source. Charity is God's gift of himself that touches and surpasses our efforts to do what is right. We must allow ourselves therefore to be overcome by love and put no obstacle in the way of the four new dimensions of God's love imparted to our souls that are thus energised and enriched to exercise virtue. St Paul describes these dimensions as 'the breadth, length, height and depth', recognised by the saints in the Cross and expressed in the love of God, of Christ, and of his disciples."

I pray that the Lord will bless you and pour out upon you that great spirit which in everything tends to the perfection and infinity for which we have been created. According to God's plan, we wait upon him in our nothingness for everything that is truly good without exception. So we have to raise ourselves out of the abyss of our misery by faith in the eternal and infinite goodness of our Creator, preparing ourselves for great things for his glory. He will make them known to us through obedience, and enable us to carry them out as perfectly as possible. Above all I would like you to be characterised by unlimited charity and the prayer which is its root and nourishment.

(*Fr Antonio Rosmini, Letters to his Brethren*)

Antonio in Rome and Gaeta

In 1848 the King of Piedmont-Sardinia, Carlo Alberto di Savoia, selected Antonio to undertake a delicate diplomatic mission to Rome to ask Pius IX to sanction a concordat between the Church and Piedmont, and approve a confederation of Italian states under Papal presidency. Such a cause was in accord with Antonio's hope that Rome would become the capital of a new unified Italy but, no sooner had Pius given him a warm and trusting welcome, than a dramatic change occurred. A new government in Piedmont altered the brief of the proposed concordat and confederation, stipulating that the Papal States join them in a war against Austria and drive Austrian forces from Italy. This was not in Antonio's mandate and he withdrew from his diplomatic appointment, but such were his abilities that Pius asked him to remain in Rome.

The Pope appointed him to join senior bishops as a consultor to deliberate on the definability of the Immaculate Conception of the Blessed Virgin Mary; this was eventually declared an article of faith in the apostolic constitution *Ineffabilis Deus* of 8th December 1854. On 15th November 1848, Rome was thrown into turmoil by the assassination of the Prime Minister of the Papal States.

The Church

'Individual members of the faithful do not immolate the Victim of the New Testament through the consecration of bread and wine, but they are able to offer it to the Eternal Father by uniting themselves in spirit with the holocaust of propitiation for the salvation of the world. All the prayers and actions they offer acquire a special value and efficacy through the priestly character they possess.'

(Fr Antonio Rosmini)

Taking part in the Eucharistic Sacrifice which is the fount and apex of the Christian life, they offer the divine Victim to God, and offer themselves along with it. By the act of oblation and through Holy Communion, they perform their part in a personal way. Strengthened anew at the holy table by the Body of Christ, they manifest in a practical way the unity of God's people brought about in this most wonderful Sacrament.

(Lumen Gentium n.11)

Antonio was nominated as the next Cardinal Secretary of State and Minister of Education, and was invited to serve as Prime Minister of the Papal States. He declined, because he felt the Pope was under duress from politicians intent on limiting papal autonomy and, though he favoured emancipation from Austria, he preferred a confederation of the Italian states under Papal authority to any other form of political unification.

To Gaeta

Nine days later, on 24th November a Roman Republic was declared and Pope Pius withdrew to Gaeta, accompanied by Antonio on whose advice he still depended. The situation was complicated by Cardinal Giacomo Antonelli who strongly supported Austria, and was eager to use foreign troops to defend the Church's temporal power. This was contrary to Antonio's vision of social and juridical reform, and he incurred the displeasure of the Cardinal by saying so. In February 1849, an elected assembly in Rome voted for the Roman Republic to be placed under the leadership of a soldier of fortune, Giuseppe Garibaldi. Later in the year, Austria's victory over Piedmont restored Austrian rule in northern Italy, and a French army overthrew the Roman Republic and restored Papal authority, at least for the time being. Antonio was not helped by the Austrian ambassador's continued disapproval of what he regarded as Antonio's patriotic love of Italy.

Participation in the Church's Mission

The worship of God originates in the individual soul and comes to perfection when offered by the human race acting in unison. People's instinct to come together in society and share its benefits has been raised to a supernatural level by Our Lord whose grace endows it with spiritual love and unity of life in him. As St Paul says, "The blessing cup that we bless is a communion with the blood of Christ, and the bread that we break is a communion with the body of Christ. The fact that there is only one loaf means that although there are many of us, we form a single body because we all have a share in this one loaf" (cf *1 Co* 10:16-17).

(*Fr Antonio Rosmini*).

Tribulations and triumph

Those who had opposed Antonio's intellectual and philosophical writings since 1826 continued their hostility; they included a particularly vicious attack in a book sent to bishops in Rome and elsewhere asking them to persuade the Pope to condemn him and his works as heretical. Rosmini wrote to a friend, "A letter from England tells me that the Jesuits are tearing me apart without mercy, and promise that my works will soon be condemned. Many enemies take advantage to damage not only my reputation, which I have given up to the Lord in sacrifice, but also more seriously the Institute and its many works of charity." Pius IX tried to end this persecution by imposing silence on all concerned, and appointed a commission to examine Antonio's works. Despite the fact that Pius VII and Pius VIII had specifically given him the task of renewing Catholic philosophy, he humbly declared his submission and obedience to the Church. "In everything, I want to base myself on the authority of the Church, and I want the whole world to know that I adhere to this authority alone." At the time, Giovanni Manzi, a young man studying for the priesthood, met Antonio and later wrote of him, "Although Rosmini's troubles were at their height, one would never had thought it to look at him, always affable and smiling. I believe he was internally happy." Perhaps Giovanni knew that one of Antonio's favourite messages St Paul sends to all of us is "There is no need to worry; but if there is anything you need, pray for it, asking God for it with prayer and thanksgiving, and that peace of God, which is so much greater than we can understand, will guide your hearts and your thoughts, in Christ Jesus" (*Ph* 4:6-7).

Not all Jesuits were opposed to Antonio. Indeed, many thought very highly of him and regretted the treatment he received. Father Peter-Hans Kolvenbach's observations mentioned in the Introduction were in the context of regret for previous animosity and, in 2008, the Jesuit Cardinal Carlo Maria Martini, former Archbishop of Milan, attended the General Congregation of the Institute of Charity. There he spoke of his admiration for the Rosminians and his sadness at Antonio's past treatment. At the same time, Father Liberti, who was then the Jesuit Provincial in Italy, asked the Holy See to accelerate the cause of Antonio's beatification.

Books forbidden

When Antonio decided the time had come for him to leave Rome, he went to stay for a while with his friend Cardinal Tosti in Albano. In November 1849, while travelling through northern Italy on his way home to Stresa, distressing news reached him. Two of his works, *The Five Wounds of Holy Church* and *The Civil Constitution according to Social Justice*, had been placed on the *Index of Forbidden Books* as containing material contrary to faith and morals. To make things worse, the Pope had previously appointed him a Consultor to the Congregation in charge of these decisions; Pius IX had seen him three days before the decree was signed but had not told him. *The Five Wounds* was particularly censured for the expressed opinions that the Church suffered from defects in the exercise of their respective priesthood by the priest and people at worship, in the education of ordained ministers, in failures of collegiality among bishops, and in the use of the Church's material wealth.

The Good and Faithful Servant

Antonio was only fifty-two, but had aged beyond his years; his hair was white and the poor health that had afflicted him in adult life was now exacerbated by painful intestinal disorders, but he was still serene and at peace. Supported by his friends, including the author Alessandro Manzoni, he continued to serve God during these last years in Stresa, giving guidance to his two religious orders and writing his supreme metaphysical work, *Theosophy*, about the mutually reasonable and advantageous relationship between philosophy and religion. It was an endeavour much in keeping with what Pope Pius VIII had asked of him in 1830 when he was in his prime. At the request of Cardinal Recanati, he also wrote *On Theological*

God and self

God presents himself to us in his gifts and teaches us how we can be present with our spirit and personality in all that we try to do for him and for our neighbour. When we are sad that we have neglected prayer or not been present in spirit, even after we have assisted at Mass, we have to accept our recognised limitations with humility. Such an experience may apply even when our attempt to do good for our neighbour has been half-hearted or unsympathetic. Then we must remember that God works in everything that exists and that his presence ensures full and perfect activity. This we can imitate by doing our best to use the talents he has given us in his service, including the power to suffer. We can grasp the significance of what Our Lord says, "Whoever would save his life in this world will lose it, and whoever loses his life for my sake and the Gospel's will save it". Love finds all its delight in the beloved; loving self means losing self, but he who recognises that delight in self is his enemy will save his life in this world by renouncing absolute self-complacency (cf. Mt 16:25; Mk 8:35; Jn 12:25).

(*Fr Antonio Rosmini*)

Language, but both works remained unfinished because, as it was said, "his sufferings prevented his writing keeping pace with his mind."

The Joy of the Lord

Early in 1854, Antonio's writings were officially tried by the Vatican for the first time. On 3rd July Pius IX presided over a general meeting of Consultors and eight Cardinals. He condemned "the cowardly, ignoble and vulgar attacks without a trace of charity on a man worthy of great respect". In their ensuing Decree "Dimittantur" the Consultors pronounced that "their examination in no way detracts from the good name of the author, nor of the Religious Society founded by him, nor from his life and singular merits towards the Church." While the Decree gave no positive approval, it guaranteed that the examined writings of Antonio contained nothing to be censured and could be read with safety. The Pope conveyed the decision privately to the Jesuits and to Antonio. The news was a timely comfort to Antonio Rosmini; on 1st July 1855, the Feast of the Most Precious Blood, God called him to his reward, at the early age of fifty-eight. In his final hours, friends asked him "What shall we do without you?" His characteristic reply was, "Adore, be silent, rejoice." His body rests in the church of the Sanctissimo Crocifisso that he built at Stresa, and in 1896 the city of Milan erected a magnificent monument and statue to his memory.

Co-operation in the Redemption

The redemption and salvation of the entire human race is entirely the work of Our Lord Jesus Christ who sacrificed himself, shed his blood for us upon the Cross, and asks us to cooperate with him in the final completion of universal redemption. He has founded his Church, the Mystical Body of which he is the head, so that the efforts we make and the good we accomplish will be to the benefit of every member. We share in the saints' power to offer prayer of intercession accompanied by a good life that is pleasing to God. Even if we feel unworthy because of our offences, our prayer is still our valuable contribution to redemption. In his goodness, God chooses to call each of us to participate in the work of redemption that Our Lord has completely achieved without need of anyone, but his great love for us impels him to make us his ministers. He sent the Apostles to make disciples of all the nations, to baptise them in the name of the Father, the Son, and Holy Spirit, and teach them to observe his commandments, and this work is required of all of us until the end of time when the whole world is brought into relationship with him. The apostolate of the Mystical Body is directed to the attainment of this goal and continued by the Church through her members so that, by its nature, the Christian vocation is a vocation to the apostolate. (*Fr Antonio Rosmini*)

Justification at last

Nearly a generation later, in 1876, argument arose again because some people contended that the decree "Dimittantur" was ambiguous, and that it was not the examination that had been "dismissed" but the writings; and that they were, in fact, open to criticism and censure. In 1887, Pope Leo XIII was swayed by this opinion, condemned forty propositions drawn from Antonio's writings, and forbade their being taught.

However, after many years of being suspected of heresy, Antonio emerged from the shadows during the period of the Second Vatican Council, and *The Five Wounds* was widely appreciated by the Council Fathers. In 1972, Pope Paul VI said at a General Audience, "Rosmini was a great man, too little known today. His spirit and thinking should be made known and imitated, and perhaps, he himself should be invoked as a protector in heaven. We look forward eagerly to the day when that will happen."

On 1st July 2001, the anniversary of Antonio's death, the Congregation for the Doctrine of the Faith led by Cardinal Joseph Ratzinger, later Pope Benedict XVI, revoked all condemnation of him. With this development, the cause for Antonio's beatification continued apace. On 26th June 2006, Pope Benedict signed the decree declaring his heroic virtue, declared him Venerable and, on 3rd June 2007, authorised his beatification. Antonio was proclaimed Blessed on Sunday, 18th November 2007, in the northern

Italian diocese of Novara in which he had lived his final years. This seems a good moment to record one of Blessed Antonio's poems:

How delightful it is to speak with God, to talk of God, to be satisfied with God alone;
To recall, desire, understand, know and love God;
To seek and find God in God,
giving oneself wholly to God.
To leave for the sake of God even the delights of God;
To think, to speak, to work for God;
To hope only in God, delight only in God,
to keep one's mind always intent on God;
To do all things with God in God,
dedicated and consecrated to God,
Pleasing God alone, suffering for God,
rejoicing solely in God;
To desire God alone,
to abide with God for ever;
To exult with God in times of joy,
in times of pain;
To see, touch, taste God, to live,
die and abide in God,
And then, rapt and translated into God,
With God and in God, to offer God to God for God's eternal honour and glory. (Fr Antonio Rosmini)

A philosopher for all seasons

When Antonio wrote his philosophical works for the Church at the behest of two Popes, he looked to restore the balance between reason and religion that had been distorted by the Enlightenment movements. His aims and methods embraced the notions of natural theology and "being", the dignity and freedom of the human person, morality, human rights, the nature of society, the objectivity of thought, and the concept of certainty. He wanted "to systematise truth and eradicate error, to offer a philosophy that would complement theology and sustain branches of knowledge that would include politics, cosmology, education, psychology, science and art". He produced a veritable encyclopaedia of harmonious ideas co-ordinated to help human beings live fruitfully on earth and achieve their spiritual destiny. He explains in *Theodicy*, "If philosophy is to be appreciated again with love and respect, I think it will be necessary to return to the teaching of the ancients and give these the benefit of modern methods." With St Augustine and St Thomas Aquinas as his guides, he teaches that God has placed in human nature the universal idea of "being". The gift of reason, he maintains, helps us understand the fundamental principle of philosophy, and the criterion of truth and beauty. He shares his appreciation of philosophy, which is "the science of ultimate reasons and grounds of human knowledge that points us to truth and helps us avoid error. Of course, mistakes are made because the answer one finds to a question at level 'A' for example, may not necessarily solve it at level 'B', so the philosopher addresses problems that arise in succeeding generations, and then formulates questions that help find solutions. The process can never be perfect and we can misjudge situations, but perseverance helps to avoid error."

Continuing care

With wonderful foresight, Antonio reminds us of Christianity's tradition that there is no tension between faith and reason. In his day, the two had become separated, but he affirmed with St Augustine that "believers are also thinkers; in believing they think and in thinking they believe. If faith does not think, it can slip into myth and superstition." When he speaks of branches of knowledge as allies of faith rather than opponents, he transcends his own time as a universal mentor whose teaching remains applicable to every age. He is, therefore recommended by Pope St John Paul II in his encyclical *Fides et Ratio* ("Faith and Reason") of 1998: "We see the fruitful relationship between philosophy and the word of God in the courageous research pursued by recent thinkers like Antonio Rosmini and John Henry Newman."

The dignity of the human person

Naming some of Antonio's works does little justice to his prolific accomplishment, but they include a *Treatise on Moral Conscience*, a *New Essay on the Origin of Ideas*, *The Principles of Modern Science*, *The Restoration of Philosophy*, *The Philosophy of Right*, *The Constitution under Social Justice*, *Maxims of Christian Perfection*, and the *Philosophy of Law*. In this last he expressed his primary political concern, which was to protect the dignity and liberty of the human person, and to recognise the positive relationship between private property and individual freedom. "Property," he said, "constitutes a sphere around the person upon which no one else should encroach, and is a defence against state intrusion and oppressive, dictatorial and pseudo-democratic regimes. Freedom is the power one possesses to use all one's faculties and resources without invading the rights of others. Property is the union of goods with the human personality in a bond that is physical, intellectual and moral. The moral bond protects the other two because the moral law forbids one person to take from another what he has united to himself by affection and intelligence." He shared St Alphonsus Liguori's opinion that, "If there is a doubt regarding the existence of a positive law that cannot be resolved, then there is no obligation; but if there is a doubt in a matter relating to the natural law and relating to an evil that is inherent in

Abide in Me

Christ the divine person communicates divinity to human nature he has joined to himself, and human beings are granted a perception of this divinity through baptism and the grace of faith. This infinite action puts the individual in touch with divinity and helps him understand the duty to submit to a dominion in which he finds all good. In this cooperation with grace, God continues his sanctifying work and guides the individual's actions. "Abide in me and I in you…I am the vine, you are the branches. Whoever remains in me, with me in him, bears fruit in plenty". The good that is characteristic of the divine nature is united to that which belongs to human nature. The greatest good is the divine nature possessed and enjoyed identically by Father and Son in such a way that Christ can say to his Father "We are One" (cf. Jn 15:4-5, 17:22).

(Fr Antonio Rosmini)

In the human nature which he united to himself, the Son of God redeemed man and transformed him into a new creation. By communicating his spirit to his brethren, called together from all peoples, Christ made them mystically into his own Body.

(Lumen Gentium, n.7)

an action, the risk of the evil must be avoided." Today we can recall that he was most attentive to the sufferings and difficulties endured by the poor and disadvantaged, and that he reminds us that any assistance the State might give does not absolve us from the duty of charitable concern and additional contribution.

Care for the Church

Antonio's *The Five Wounds of Holy Church* was written in just ten days towards the end of November 1832. He drew attention to the dangers that threatened Church unity and freedom and suggested how these might be averted. As previously intimated, his worries included the absence of unity among bishops; the nomination of bishops by some European political powers; infringement upon church property; and the lack of communication between clergy and people, particularly in matters of public worship. He knew that many people found it difficult to participate fully in the liturgy and rejoice in the sacramental life of the Church, not just because of the Latin that was then exclusively used in the liturgy, but because they had not been adequately instructed in the Faith. He believed resurgence would come from a renewed appreciation of prayer and the Mass, where attendance is not as an audience, but as a participation in Our Lord's saving work of Redemption. Doubtless he will have interceded for his fellow priests recently as they introduced their parishioners to the new translation of the *Roman Missal*, and explained the benefits of attending the sacred rituals. He anticipated the Second Vatican Council's 'Decree on the Ministry and Life of Priests': "Priests should teach the people to participate in the celebrations of the sacred liturgy in such a way that they can rise to sincere prayer in them…Let them take care to cultivate an appropriate knowledge and facility in the liturgy, so that by their own liturgical ministry, the Christian communities entrusted to them may ever more adequately give praise to God, the Father and the Son and the Holy Spirit" (n.5).

Support for the Clergy

Antonio sympathised with secular clergy of the day who found it difficult to instruct people because their seminary training had been based on digestible modules rather than serious study of the Scriptures and the teaching of the Fathers and Doctors of the Church, especially St Thomas Aquinas. Like great shepherds such as St Charles Borromeo and St Francis de Sales, he thought that education for the priesthood would be better served if aspirants lived with their bishops rather than isolated in seminaries. Perhaps he would sympathise with modern secular clergy, who are often classified as "self-employed" and, after ordination and appointment, may not experience any community life which can support them as they deal with the complex experiences of contemporary life.

The importance of the hierarchy

The Second Vatican Council declared that bishops play a key role in the Church and the lives of her children. Antonio wondered if there might be some advantage in a return to the ancient tradition in which the people and clergy of a diocese elected their bishop; after all, the names of great pastors like St Ambrose and St Augustine had been put forward by those they were to serve. He respected bishops as prophets, fathers, and pastors who speak with one voice, not as civil servants selected by secular states and thus subject to political whim. The Church must be free from state interference, allowed to control her own property, and be recognised as separate from, though co-operating with, the state. These views now form the basis for the Church's current teaching on social questions, and the Second Vatican Council heeded his advice on how the Church should respond to the needs of society, undertake her legitimate civic responsibilities, and fulfil Our Lord's wish that she should teach all nations. Antonio can be heard when the Fathers of the Council comment: "In exercising his office as father and pastor, a bishop should stand in the midst of his people as one who serves. Let him be a good shepherd who knows his sheep and whose sheep know him. Let him be a true father who excels in the spirit of love and solicitude for all, and to whose divinely conferred authority all gratefully submit themselves. Let him so gather and mould the whole family of his flock so that everyone, conscious of his own duties, may live and work in the communion of love. He should always welcome priests with a special love since they share in his duties and zealously carry the weight of these every day. He should regard them as sons and friends, listen to them, and so promote the work of the diocese" (*Christus Dominus*, (On the Pastoral Office of Bishops), n.16).

A Light to the Church

In the tradition of the Catholic Church's great political theorists, Antonio tirelessly defended the freedom of citizens from abuses that might be perpetrated by an all-powerful state. He was impressed by the thesis of *Democracy in America* written by his contemporary Alexis de Tocqueville and, like him, saw no essential tension between liberalism and religion. He pioneered the beneficial relationship of faith and liberalism with charitable sensitivity to the human predicament, and many would claim that Church leaders have often drawn on his erudite thinking. He saw that the order of the universe God has created is reflected in human beings and is the basis of the essential dignity in their rights to life, to a just wage, to freedom of worship and to form associations. "These rights with their accompanying duties contribute to the effective establishment of a society in which they are fulfilled." By more than a century, he anticipated Pope St John XXIII's 1963 encyclical *Pacem in Terris* ('Peace on Earth'), which recalls his definition of rights and duties, a definition that now characterises Catholic social teaching. It prepared the way for the Second Vatican Council's Declaration on Religious Freedom (*Dignitatis Humanae*) that sought "to develop the doctrine on the inviolable rights of the human person and the constitutional order of society." For the first time, official Catholic teaching acknowledged the validity of religious pluralism, the responsibility of government in protecting and promoting human rights and duties, and the Church's position as "the fundamental principle in what concerns the relations between Church, government, and the whole civil order." Many other Decrees of the Second Vatican Council reveal an appreciation of Antonio's research, scholarship and spirituality.

Priestly Formation

Catholic life depends on a generous response to God's call to the ministerial priesthood, and the words of the Fathers of the Council remind us of *The Five Wounds of Holy Church*. "We confide to seminary directors and teachers the duty of forming Christ's future priests, and entreat those preparing for the priestly ministry to realise that the hope of the Church and the salvation of souls is entrusted to them. Priestly training should be pursued and perfected even after the seminary course of studies has been completed, and Episcopal Conferences should use the most effective procedures available, for example, pastoral institutes, conferences, and projects to introduce younger clergy to apostolic activity and to develop their priestly lives. Let teachers reverently pay heed to the voice of the Doctors of the Church, among whom St Thomas holds the principal place. His teaching is efficacious in safeguarding the foundations of the Faith and reaping the fruits of its progress" (*Optatam Totius* n.16 & n. 22).

Antonio's 'Maxims of Christian Perfection'

To desire without limit to please God, that is, to be just.

To direct all one's thoughts and actions to the increase and glory of the Church of Jesus Christ.

To remain in perfect peace as God orders events, whatever happens to ourselves, or even to the Church, and to follow God's call in working for the Church.

To abandon oneself wholly to the care of Divine Providence.

To acknowledge profoundly one's own nothingness.

To direct all the actions of one's life with prayer to the Holy Spirit for the gifts of understanding and wise counsel.

(*Fr Antonio Rosmini*)

Acknowledgements

The writer wishes to thank Father John Daley and Father Anthony Dewhirst of the Institute of Charity without whose wise counsel this appreciation of a "Prophet for the Third Millennium" could not have been completed.

Recourse to the following sources is gratefully acknowledged.

The Life of Antonio Rosmini. Turin, Institute of Charity, 1897.

Rosminian Spirituality: In the Spirit of the Founder. Guys, Cardiff, Institute of Charity, 1970.

Chadwick, Owen, *History of Christianity*. London, Weidenfeld & Nicolson, 1995.

Cleary IC, D *Antonio Rosmini: Introduction to his Life and Teaching*. Durham, Rosmini House, 1992.

Dewhirst IC, J A, *Antonio Rosmini and the Fathers of the Church*. Exeter, Short Run Press, 2005.

Dewhirst IC, J A, *Our Light and Our Salvation*. Exeter, Short Run Press, 2009.

Johnson, Paul, *The Papacy*. London, Weidenfeld & Nicolson, 1997.

Sheehan, M, *Apologetics and Christian Doctrine*. London, Saint Austin Press, 2001.